Don't Trust Me

AF497071

Harry Stagaman

BookLeaf
Publishing

India | USA | UK

Presentation by *BookLeaf Publishing*

Web: www.bookleafpub.com

E-mail: info@bookleafpub.com

ISBN: 9789358319545

First edition 2024

To Nat

Thank you for always trusting me.

ACKNOWLEDGEMENT

Thank you to Bookleaf Publishing for the opportunity to showcase my work.

Thank you to my family for their constant support of me in all forms. I appreciate the read-throughs, the jokes, and the endless amounts of love that I carry with me in every word.

Thank you to my countless readers: Ella, Anneliese, Alyssa, Celia, and Nat. Your perspective and comments shaped this work and brought a level of care that I deeply appreciate.

Thank you Halli for taking part in this journey alongside me. Your writing is endlessly inspiring to me, and I'm ecstatic that we can celebrate the beauty of our own words alongside each other.

Amid the mud

I am slipping
and everyone is leaving me behind.
they march on.
paths already set
and I'm left to stir in the mud.
Its deep layers of unknown
grip and strangle,
freezing me in purgatory.

Grown

I don't like my hair
short like this.

Easier to maintain,
sure,
but it's a faulty frame.

My head shape bulky,
the curls out of order.

Too stubby to place
over my eyes,
and too flimsy to hold

its shape. I can't
hide in it, absorb into

the volume of the
homegrown rusted gold:
An expired currency.

I pull to stretch it out,
but growth isn't that simple.

Haven

The stench of the porch carpet
branches into my lungs.
Filling my body;
in and out.

Odors of rubber and heat simmer
as I lay in the sun's light;
the breeze too cold,
the light too hot.

Home always has a way of
opposing.
Fixing for a hug,
failing to hold me.

The songs of barking and
bickering jerk me back.
The room sickens me.
Must be the stench.

Don't trust me

My nails keep breaking.
Snapping into shards that slice my skin
and pierce my eyes.

I whittle them down,
as dull as the world without me.
The shaved-down dust more valuable than diamond.

I flick through my list
of potential sources of pleasure; a repertoire
of irrational lovers that I can feed on.

I'm their best person: a vial of light.
Little do they know of my poisonous trail,
lined with the graves of each obligatory embrace.

Love can be measured; I drink every ounce.
So much to steal, more than enough to strip from
every hollow heart to lay in my hand.

It's always their fault: the fallout.
Each scar of decayed devotion sealed
in the locket upon my chest.

Trust is a tool; easy to acquire
when a smile is so coaxing and
promises so palpable.

Adoration injected into my veins,
the high, my only fuel.
Taken from the hands of the naive.

Unkept

The coffee table is a mess.
Littered with old candies and
magazines we should have
recycled months ago.

I swipe off the crumbs
and rearrange the collage
of collectibles.
Condensing the eyesore.

Two wine glasses linger.
One stained with your fingerprints;
unable to be emulated.
I leave them as a souvenir.

You never cared for wine.
Only sipped to simulate some
sort of synergy.
That we clicked;

but the false connection
could only be maintained for
so long until the mess piled up.
Leaving me to clean.

Check, please

I got a call from
the bank. I've been
spending more recently.
I didn't realize.

My wallet slimming down
as I run through my statement,
piecing back each time
I left my card off-leash.

Coffees with friends to
empty out my sour
pitcher of misery; clothing items
to revolutionize my look

that didn't fit quite right;
emergency meals that sickened
me; nights of euphoria
that shamed me the next

morning. All fleeting moments
of bliss to keep the waves of
aimless angst at bay. The feeling
lingers, but the cash is gone.

Let go

I don't like my face
right now.

My cheeks are larger.
I've stopped my regular
bursts of cardio weeks ago.

It's caught up to me.

My clothes still fit,
I still catch looks, but
I can't look in the mirror
the same way.

I detest my waist,
my arms,
my ass.

I let them slip.
Left to be unsightly.

Dwindle

It feels I should go
for a long time.

Somewhere,
anywhere,
as long as I'm gone.

No longer prying,
speaking,
hurting,
crying.

Building a new path;
free from

everything.

Pastimes

The room is still but
a quiet buzzing from
the vents is keeping
my mind active; almost
singing a tune that I try to
decipher so I can harmonize,
and I vocalize alongside but it
muddles into groans as I exult my
limited energy from twisting and
tightening my lanky limbs while
pacing my way across the
clothing-covered floors of
this false sanctuary, besides,
I am free here among the
constrictions of my four
blessed walls with the world
as my oyster; this bedroom,
the pearl I hold tightly against
my slow-beating heart, with
its photo-covered walls
showcasing the items of
idealization that kept my
roaring engine of ambitions
purring amongst the
frequent flair-ups of failure

that merge their way into
my freeway of fantasies,
and I take in the anthology
of adorations; flashing back
to memories that housed
me in an expanse of liberation-
induced blunders that beckoned
me back into the storyteller's
chair; a life that could be listed in
order of most to least notable
instances of stupidity and
splendor, but that's all
behind me now as this room
with its dusty knick-knacks,
ghosts of lovers' past, and the
most beautiful, plain white ceiling
is all I need to feel truly satisfied;
here, I'm home.

Out of order

I can't see straight.
Everything has faded
and I wait for it to pass
but it only grows more into watercolor.
Each blink blurring the image further.

My fingers ineligible:
the deep grooves etched beneath,
marked with my missteps,
thinning down.

My head pounds.
The world an abstract idea.
I gaze through an existence
just out of grasp.
Outside of me.

What's left of me.

My retired stomach filled with nothing and everything,
plaguing my perception.
Was my last meal this afternoon
or last Tuesday?

Everything is failing
in and out.
I can feel my chest tighten,
twist,
ache.
My mind slip,
crack,

race.

Yet it all stills.
Static in contempt
because this pain
psychosis
numbness
stabilizes me.

Dusted off

I started listening
to that record you
showed me. The one
about heartbreak in California.

I only cared for one
song back when the
air gripped my throat
and shined my head like a shoe.

You always loved
the way I sang it.
Telling me it was
good enough for television.

I bet you would adore
my rendition of the
rest. Lullabies strung
from my voice and the

hardwood floors. I
finally like your
favorite track. It's
a shame it reminds me of us.

Mannequin

15

The restaurant is vacant
as old friends and I litter the
table with minor check-ins
to combat the emptiness.

It's all a ritual for us:
the pizza,
the splitting of the bill,
the repeated inside jokes,

but it's not clicking.
Not me, at least.
The car has started but
my engine sputters.

I'm a faulty part.

We press on like there's
nothing off.
As if this isn't more hollow
than our stomachs.

Jammed

I'm growing exhausted
of this chapter.

Limited action, endless misery
as the sun passes by the window
each empty afternoon.

Nothing to speak on,
the passivity of this pause

pricks away at the persistent
press of a purposeless path to
follow. I want to change,

incite something to behold,
worthy of the page's turn,

but I sink deeper into the stillness.
The pen faulty, the words impossible
to place; another moment meant to fade.

Nothing changes.
It lays, always.

Proper smile

The train is smothered
by the rush hour crowd
filtering into the rows of
shiny grey leather.

Two teenage girls settle:
talking back and forth on
the simplistic struggles
of their day to day.

One wishes she could
do a "proper smile", as if the spread
of her teeth could be anything but
something to cherish,

but they soon move on
to their peers: focusing on the
ways they could be sub-par.
Going back and forth over a classmate

that's photogenic sans her hair;
finding the cracks in others
to let the light shine on
their trees, rooted in insecurity.

Their comparison out of innocence,
unable to know of the blossoming
that comes with age, focused more
on the next stop and how to smile just right.

Idol

19

The door handle is cold.
Left unused as I stand by for someone new
to enter this life; to change this way of being.

Someone to save me from the abyss
of my own presence; make this piss-poor
existence something to cherish; to revere.

I want to be their favorite pastime.
Forever tied to each other's words, worshipping
the speeches that emerge from the mundane;

a never-ending life of sweet nothings.
Gripping us to the promises of a life tied at the bond
of two lost hands, our safe haven.

The sunlight through the window warms my skin,
but it doesn't comfort; failing to stabilize the way a
shared soul shapes my smile and waxes my worries.

My reflection, my current companion,
facing my frigid existence; the beauty unworthy for
my own face. Only in another can I be desired.

Wilted

Three summers ago,
you picked me from the fields.
Intertwined into your tangled hair,
the sunshine searing the love between.

I, your daisy, an open embrace
as you entered this world on your own.
You kept me close, buried in your pocket as
a good luck charm.

With my wisdom came your care.
Watering me with your kindness, the
sunshine pouring out of your smile.
Each day in your grasp bringing me closer to the clouds,

but now the shine has faded;
left to reside on your bedside table.
The forest more promising to you,
my limited beauty less gripping.

My petals frail as paper,
my stem slouching to the Earth.
Your hair tightly wound, flowers a
souvenir of naivety.

The floral age falling out of style.
My all, now a memory of self-discovery.
The promise of better in your grasp,
and I lay here, bloomless.

Reissued

The dark has crept
into the afternoon and
the cold has settled into
the alleyways.

Winter has perched its place
amongst the trees and the early
morning chill, festering into the
fears of my absolution.

Its frigid return resides on my
cheeks; my face shifting to
porcelain, the fragility seeping
into my malleable demeanor.

I turn to winters prior,
housing the flimsy shells of my phony
contentment. My obituary revised
each night as my eyes sealed.

Every passing moment failed to
nourish my active corpse.
The joy of living turned dark as
snow shifted to slush.

The flakes fall,
their beauty fading into the fickle
remains of my false hopes.
The season seizes,
and I submit.

In every step

I knew I shouldn't have done it:
stayed with you
deep in your grasp.
Your cold touch wrapped around me.

Dropping my temperature
as I tried to get through it;
through you.

I seared my eyes shut;
unable to give myself fully
and you persisted.

Scratches on my face;
enough to hurt,
but never deep enough to bleed.

Stuck in all of you;
inescapable,
and all I want is to be away,
but I feel you in my lungs.
On my skin.
In my mouth.

The smell of you lingers on my clothes.

Seeped into the fabric
as I lay
frozen from your touch,

and I know I'll join you again.
I only saw you on a bad day,
and surely, it will be better next time.

Cherub

The steam rises from
my freshly poured coffee.
The bubbles bouncing at the surface
of the bitter, brown sea.

Mom's spoon scats as she
cycles it in circles; mixing the
cream and sweetener to salvage
the flavor for her palette.

She was just telling me how
I was the sweetest little boy;
how I was so cute that everyone
wanted to eat me up;

noting that she still sees that
sweetness in me, even as I ingest the
grim flavors of maturity in my mug.
I don't blame her; it seems

most see that innocence.
Taking each grain of sugar they can
squeeze out of me; making the bitterness
easier to swallow.

My smile, easy to grasp.
My efforts in the wrong hands.
The best in others, all a ruse,
as disappointment feeds.

Commute

I took the train one
stop further this time.
I wanted to walk

along the streets
under the lampposts
and soak in the air.

The rosy tingles into
my cheeks with each passing
kiss of the wind.

Every step booms
against the shiny asphalt
as the rain lingers along

the dimly lit stretch.
The smell of Earth and time
reach to the faded starlight.

I retrace the path
my old footprints laid between
the breaks of the sidewalk.

I continue, home within reach.

Muscle memory guiding as my aimless
psyche convolutes.

28

Cocooned

I can feel the walls
weaken, the confines of
this cocoon thinning down.

Genuine joy defrosting as
I walk the grocery store.
Gasping at the seasonal sweets.

Laughter comes more naturally.
The air finally releasing;
Holding in, no more.

The steam of tea filling the air,
a weightless companion for this newfound
groundedness; weighted.

The faults of my own thinking
still stray along, finding ways to
sliver into the cracks,

but they no longer echo.
Freed from my isolation chamber,
I can see the expanses.

Warmth in everything I gaze upon:

dancing branches of the trees,
photographs of forgotten loves,
the moments of my own presence;
forever precious.

Sprouting anew, a life of promise
in the palm of my own hands.
Everything is mine for the taking,

all that's left is to fly.